Call *On* God

Marvin S. Ross

Call On God

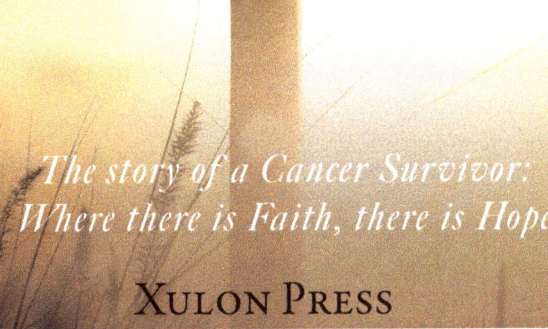

*The story of a Cancer Survivor:
Where there is Faith, there is Hope*

XULON PRESS

Xulon Press
2301 Lucien Way #415
Maitland, FL 32751
407.339.4217
www.xulonpress.com

© 2023 by Marvin S. Ross

All rights reserved solely by the author. The author guarantees all contents are original and do not infringe upon the legal rights of any other person or work. No part of this book may be reproduced in any form without the permission of the author.

Due to the changing nature of the Internet, if there are any web addresses, links, or URLs included in this manuscript, these may have been altered and may no longer be accessible. The views and opinions shared in this book belong solely to the author and do not necessarily reflect those of the publisher. The publisher therefore disclaims responsibility for the views or opinions expressed within the work.

Paperback ISBN-13: 978-1-66288-052-0
Ebook ISBN-13: 978-1-66288-053-7

This is my life story of loving God, the power of prayer, surviving cancer 5 times over a twenty-two-year period, and the prayer warriors across America who gave strength.

Dedication

To my wife and rock, Mary Ann Rankin Ross. To my daughters and granddaughter; Christie, Melissa, and Samantha. To my Aunt Peggy and Aunt Esper (Mom's sisters), my Pastor Wendell, my friend and mentor; John A. (Chicago Police officer, Wood Street station), Mike and Fredric Attorneys at Law.

Table of Contents

Chapter 1.
Five-time Cancer survivor 1

Chapter 2.
I ask, "Can I fight for my country?" 5

Chapter 3.
Mary Rankin & Family, My Rock 11

Chapter 4.
After 10 years cancer is back.. 23

Chapter 5.
Deer VS Bike Harley Trip around Lake Michigan 33

Chapter 6.
Eight Day, Trouble in river city 41

Chapter 7.
Brain cancer 49

Chapter 8.
Cancer returns, Brain cancer. 55

Chapter 9.
People that I admire.. 61

Chapter 1

Five-Time Cancer Survivor

Having survived cancer five times I firmly believe that miracles can happen. Where there is faith there is hope. There is always a chance for healing. Find your support system whether it's family, friends, or medical professionals, and surround yourself with people that love you and care for you. That will get you through it. You need Prayer warriors who recognize the action by coming before God; God calls on believers to fight in spiritual battles that are constantly taking place.

It is Christmas Eve, 1958. My brother Robert, who was around one and a half years old at the time and I (four years old) had decided to find our Christmas gifts. For some reason, I had no idea about Santa Claus. We lived in a house that was behind a three-story apartment building. Our home ran along the back of an alley around Foster and Broadway in Chicago. Ms. Schumann was the owner of the property. Robert and I were looking in the closets to find our Christmas gifts. We went to the small pantry next to the kitchen. I opened the door "Wow" there were the toys." My dad had just come home from the Korean War; he grew up in Delaware, and he had met my mom at a roller rink in North Carolina "Fort Bragg." He was told Chicago is where you can make big money to raise a family. My two aunts and their husbands moved with us to Chicago. We had a part of our family around the Chicago area. My dad had PTSD and Doctors were never able to resolve his problems, another story for later.

Robert and I had opened the door, there were the toys. I'm not so happy not because of the toys, just depressed. In front of me is a wall, it opens "IT

IS GOD" I know him. I ask, "Why am I back here?" No words from GOD, just a smile. I knew then all would be well, for me, my Bother, and the future. Three years later another brother was born, David. Three years after David my sister Yulanda. We were all 3 years apart.

We moved From Forster and Broadway to 737 N. Hoyne St, west side of Chicago. It is between Chicago Ave and Damen Ave. We were in poverty. We were children and did not know it. We thought we were rich. Then Dad lost his job and started stealing milk from ice boxes off the steps of peoples' homes. The ice boxes were provided for those who had dairy products delivered to their home by Deans Milk Dairy company. The milk boxes were outside in front of the door of the properties. Mr. Lupo caught my dad around 5 am in the morning. He told my dad to put it back. When Dad got caught by Mr. Lupo, that is when he decided to finally tell Mr. Lupo about his misfortune. My Dad told Mr. Lupo I will not be able to pay my rent this month, Mr. Lupo, I lost my job. Mr. Lupo was a good man, we lived on the south end of the first floor of a three-story with six apartments in the building that he owned.

Years have gone by; we had our ups and downs like all the families in our neighborhood. However, we all supported each other, emotionally and financially. On my first day of school in the classroom I saw a few Black children. When I got home, I said Mom there are children with Black skin. She said do not fret that in a thousand years, we will all be the same. To always be kind and nice to others. We don't know what others are going through. They're just like us. They have a mom and dad that work hard to make a living, and they go to school to learn the same things we do for a better life, a smile, and a kind word can change a person's day.

I was around eight years old, and my brother David was three, and we somehow caught Hepatitis C. My mom thought it was just a cold until we were so sick, we were not able to get out of bed. Mr. Lupo demanded that Mom take us to Cook County Hospital. We had no money, no health insurance, he drove us there. Back then there was no cure, just hope and rest.

The Doctor told my mom David was not so bad however Marvin probably will not survive. We were placed in the contagious disease ward. The room was about 20' X 20', like a small apartment. It had everything we needed. Concrete walls halfway up, glass all around with a locked door to keep an eye on us. We stayed in that room for about eight or ten weeks or so, David was well in about 3 weeks. The Doctors left him in there just so I would not be alone. My family had a very deep religious Baptist Pentecostal faith. Their mission statement was the Holy Spirit and the believer's direct experience of the presence of GOD. Pentecostals believed that faith must be powerfully defined and not something found merely through ritual or thinking. Pentecostalism is energetic and dynamic. My grandmother was a Pentecostal Pastor in Lincolnton North Carolina.

My mom had this friend, I cannot remember her name, but her husband was a Heroin addict and would beat her all the time. He had caught Spinal Meningitis and died not before giving it to his wife. My mom insisted that she should leave her husband and live with us. She worked at night and slept in my bed during the day. David and I caught Spinal Meningitis, yep, this time my eyes were yellow blood color to include David also. Again, we were so sick with fever and headaches our eyes hurt looking into the light. Back to Cook County Hospital contagious disease ward. Doctors said again, this time I was around eleven, that I would not survive Spinal Meningitis. Once again, no cure was available at that time. David survived and recovered in about four weeks this time. He stays with me another eight weeks or so. We were back in the contagious disease ward, that same room again. I survived; GOD IS GOOD. I believed and had Faith; the truth is I had no idea what was happening. With faith there is always hope my mom would always say; all a person needs is faith the size of a mustard seed and they can move a mountain. I believed everything my mom told us.

I was fourteen and a half years old that summer, I would sneak on the bus and then the L-train; I had no money. I would go from the west side of Chicago to Broadway and Foster Ave. to meet up with my cousin Iris Bell and her friends. It was a teen church with lots of music and a younger pastor. This is where I gave my life to GOD and asked for his forgiveness and love.

This is Iris 3rd to the right and her three daughters.

The neighborhood boys

The neighborhood boys, there were two groups the good boys and the bad boys. In this Picture were the good boys and not the street gangsters. The bad boys were street gangsters, bad to the bone. There were about fifteen guys in each group. In the bad boy group, about five guys were killed by the time they were young men. A few of them were wanted by the FBI, the others more than likely jailed. We all grew up on the west side of Chicago.

Chapter 2

I ask, "Can I fight for my country."

I quit school, I wanted to be like my dad and join the Army, I was sixteen and a half years old. Army was my goal; second infantry the 104th regiment. I met with the recruiters and got my papers. I just needed them to be signed by good old Dad. Dad was so mad at me.

When I was ten, my Dad had a nervous breakdown they called "shell shock", we now know it as "PTSD". Doctors did not know how to treat "PTSD" at that time. They put my dad in a mental hospital for about a year or so. The hospital was named Dunning the county insane asylum infirmary.

My mom had to find a job ASAP; she worked all shifts to take care of us kids. My friend Avery lived next door. He helped me get a job delivering newspapers. I started a newspaper delivery route "The Tribune and the Sunday Times" with a blue tag and a red tag, a customer information tag. I still wonder today if they were Democrat and Republican tags. At the age of twelve, I needed to work to help my mom. The owner of the paper route liked to be called "Jack the Jaw." He was a true American entrepreneur. I would try to be at his storefront before anyone else. My friend Avery said if you wanted to get the good stuff be early before the other boys. I had to be there at four in the morning, in order to get the good red wagon. The wagon was important, it carried the newspapers. You had to buy rubber bands, this was a cost for me, five cents for a bag of rubber bands and fifteen cents for daily rental of the wagon. All the costs would be deducted on Sunday after the money was collected from the people that received the newspaper. We were the delivery boys and bill collectors. After Jack received the money from us and after his expenses, if we made no mistakes, the rest would be yours. All the money I made I gave to my mom to help buy food and pay bills. My mom worked like a dog.

I needed a better-paying job. My Mom had found a new Job for me delivering milk. I rode in a delivery Deans milk truck. Every morning I had to be up by three-thirty in order to get on a bus that would take me north from Chicago Ave and Damen Ave to Milwaukee Ave where there is a restaurant about fifteen miles away. I would meet Herbert, a large overweight man. He owned a Dean's delivery milk Truck. We would deliver Dean's milk and dairy; he paid me $2.00 a day Monday through Friday and $3.00 Saturday. Herbert would drop me off at Mitchell Elementary School 2233 W. Ohio ST. After school, I would work at a small restaurant washing dishes and cleaning up. On the way to and back home, I had a shoeshine box that Mr. Lupo gave me. He said this will make you some good money. He taught me how to spit-shine shoes. Turned out there were two other boys that shined shoes also. We would go into the bars from Damen Ave down Chicago Ave to Ashland Ave. However, the competitors did not like to spit shine the men's shoes, just a shine only. When I walked into the bars the men were always waiting for the boy that spit shine their shoes. They would say do not get black on my white socks. It cost twenty-five cents a shine, five cents more for a hard spit shine. All the money I made I give to my mom.

I went with my mother to see my dad at Dunning "the county insane asylum infirmary." That was the first time I saw my dad cry. He told me the most heartbreaking story ever. He told me about the second infantry 104 regiment, the first 107 men landing on the beach in amphibious assault watercraft. He told me that he was so scared but overcame the fear quickly. Before they landed on the beach, 99% of his group was killed by gunfire from the Korean army. They all died like warriors before they hit the beaches. Dad told me there were only two survivors, himself and one other. He was on the 50-Cal just shooting up the bluff at the enemy, the other man would feed the 50-Cal. He said it seemed like hours before the next infantry landed on the beach. They fought all night and all morning. In the morning it started to rain, he said there were rivers of blood coming down the bluff from all those that had died.

The American warriors made it up the bluff days later. At one point my dad was in a foxhole guarding the front lines. It was night when he fell asleep. He just woke up in time to see a young man with his Bayonet. My dad had his 45-caliber handgun in his hand as he slept, under his leg. He pulled the handgun up shot through his leg and killed the intruder. He was taken to the infirmary for treatment. He was a left-handed sharpshooter and very proficient. They patched him up and sent him back out to the front lines to be a sniper. His targets were high-ranking officers only. Then he told me the rest of his story. He did the worst thing he could ever think of doing. It did not bother him much until he found a Korean general in the enemy camp. He stayed in a tree for 3 days till a low-ranking soldier saluted another soldier then he knew he had him; now he said to himself I will shoot him. It became a game to my dad "right in the eye," and he shot and killed him. Dad told me Son I see his face and eye every day of my life. "**SON I WILL NOT SIGN THAT PAPER FOR YOU TO FIGHT,**" my dad said." SON, YOU WILL NOT GO TO WAR UNLESS IT IS GOD WILL." At that moment I understood. I remembered what he told me several years before, you will have to get your draft papers from the draft board. God will call you if he needs you, my son.

My Dad, Robert Francis Ross.

My Dad was released from Dunning, He was doing rather well and had gone back to work. Mom stayed working part-time after Dad came home. Dad said it helped to pay the bills. Dad said, after a short period, that we were going to go on a vacation. There was this dog that followed me to school and back home. He lived on my back porch under my bedroom window. I loved that dog. My dad said we could not keep the dog. Two days before we were to go on our vacation Dad gave the dog to my uncle to take care of. When we got back, the dog was gone. They told me it got hit by a car. I had anger issues. I did not treat dogs so well after that; I was heartbroken.

Where we were going would be camping and fishing. On a trip to Lac du Flambeau Wisconsin, French fur traders named the area Lac du Flambeau, "Lake of the Torches." Lush forests, abundant wildlife, 250 lakes. My Dad bought a big tent. I was fifteen and knew how to drive a little. It would be a 370-mile trip and about 8 hours from our home. Roads were slower back then; we had a family friend that hung around with us and loved fishing with my dad. Jerry was married in his twenties and drove his own car. He was the lead car on the trip. Dad was getting tired, and Mom said let Marvin drive. Wow, me, I did not even have a driver's license. We were on a back road almost to the campground. I was going around a corner and did not turn the wheel back. We went down and up off the road and got stuck on a mound. It took Jerry and Dad 2 hours to get it back on the street. No more driving for me.

It was just getting dark when we arrived at the campground, and we had the Station-Wagen loaded. Jerry's car was loaded also. They set up camp; Mom and Jerry's wife were making dinner. The next morning, I got up early. My brothers were also up. We were camping right on the beach next to the lake, forest, and trails. We were not in the concrete jungle anymore. The place was beautiful, we grab our fishing poles, and bait and fished around the beach area. We met another boy about our age. He had a small boat and asked if we would like to go out fishing with him. I did not expect that. We were out about an hour or so and we had no luck. This lake is mostly a musky lake. Robert Hooked into a big fish in about 10 minutes. The fish is at the boat, then it almost jumped in the boat. We had never seen a Musky before. I said cut the line it is an alligator. We were scared to death, but then the line broke. As soon as we got back, I ran to tell Jerry about the fish. He laughed so hard I thought he was going to wet his pants. He said there are no alligators up north; they cannot live here because it is too cold. It was a Musky and our first encounter with a monster fish. We caught a lot of fish over the next 4 days; we hated to leave.

Once we are back home Dad said, "You're going back to school;" I said no. Dad said to me, "I will not sign those Army papers." I thought Mom would sign, but that never happened, Dad was all over that. Mr. Lupo was able to get my dad his first really good job, a great job. Mr. Lupo and his family loved everybody and cared for the well-being of my family. He made my dad a union steward, and plastic setup man. The Italian people are a wonderful loving caring people. During the summer Wednesdays was spaghetti day. Mr. Lupo knew a lot of mobsters although he was not one. However, he did have power and influence. His spaghetti sauce took all day to cook. He would make about a gallon or so, and a boatload of spaghetti. At 5 o'clock he made enough to feed about twenty-five or so people on the front steps of the apartment building. He fed everybody in the neighborhood if he could. We would talk, sing, and have lots of laughter. Once a month, Friday was always pizza day for us kids; we could not wait. On pizza day Mr. Lupo made it in the basement in the wood furnace, Wow. Mr. Lupo would give his son and me twenty-five cents to get three pounds of pizza dough. When that happened, we knew it was pizza day. He said to go to Gonnella bakery boys, it was about 2 blocks away on Damen Ave and Huron St right on the corner.

One afternoon three men came by to see Mr. Lupo. They hung their guns on the hooks under the porch. "Boom" Little John and I saw them we started to reach for them when Mr. Lupo just about knocked the shit out of us. I was around thirteen and John was fourteen years old. That is when Mr. Lupo told us about this old lady with a big nose. Story goes; there was this lady with a large nose. She always looks out the door minding other people's business. Her nose stuck out the door one day she saw too much and got her nose shot off.

I told my dad no more school I will get a job, he said no you will get enrolled in a Trade school by Monday. I laughed, I already knew that Trade schools were already filled up, not for a union man's son. I took Mechanics then Journey men carpentry. In time I started a business, construction with my brother Robert. In 1973 I got married and two years later my first child Christie (1975) was born, one of the joys of my life; DAD was right.

Chapter 3

Mary Rankin & Family, My Rock

I went back to night school at Triton College, and I had taken several classes. After about 6 years or so things started working out for the best. Hard work, 12 hours a day, 6 to 7 days a week; then we started doing well. By 1987 my wife and I were finely able to take our first small Family vacation; my children's first vacation since they were born. In the summer of 1988 Tom took his Figure writer who was also a public adjuster, Robert, and me to his cabin in the north woods on a fishing trip. Wow: this was not the kind of cabin that I was thinking of; a four thousand square foot home with about five acres; you can put my home inside his garage.

I did not know it at the time, but he was grooming us for the future of his business. He helped me invest my money. He was very smart and had a talent for putting the right people in the right place. We became very good friends because we both did not mix our friendship with work, and I like it that way. We were at his cabin for about five days; he was building dreams for Robert and me. Making it known that we can have the same things he had. I knew that was not going to happen unless I was to first learn the game. I would read all the self-help books that I could get my hands on; a biography of those that I would like to be like.

Tom paid for everything that weekend. He took us out to dinner; nothing but the best. He made us breakfast and lunch, took us out fishing, and even hired a guide. That is when I started picking his brain for knowledge. Tom's figure writer shared a lot of knowledge with me. I knew that I would have to learn everything these two men knew about the restoration and adjusting business if I was to reach my full potential. However, I did not want to start as a figure writer.

There are lots of different players in this game; I was entrusted to be the chaser. The chaser is the one that shows up out of nowhere and pitches the loss. A Fire truck chaser listens to scanners, sits, and waits for the call "WE GOT A WORKING FIRE." You are in the game on the battlefield, but there are others. Faster, smarter, older, and they have more tricks than a magician. As a networking group of others pulling together for one goal; put them on paper. But before you can get in the game more school more books and a tutor. I was lucky Tom gave me all I needed to reach my goal. You see it was in his best interest; I was loyal, honest, and worked extra hours and stood by every word he said.

There was John K. a hell of a chaser that was 10 years or so older than me and a very wise African American. He had a reputation for being one of the top ten closers on the street. I had a need to be number one. He was fearless and he would walk right up to the homeowner while the building was still smoldering, and the firefighters were doing their final search and overhauling. He would say I am sorry about your fire; you are going to need some help. I can help you get the advantage over the insurance company before they get the advantage over you. I will be across the street and can talk to you in a few minutes. Either the people will ask for more information or say ok. The seed has been planted. John was a very tall African American, very smart, and had a way with people. He had no boundaries, he would pitch anyone, any race; I admired him. He was honest and did not lie to get the people to hire him; he just gave them the facts.

I was the head construction manager and did some sales. The customers would tell me their stories. There was this one time the job was done, and I had the last insurance checks to be signed. A medium built height woman with black hair about five foot nine inches tall. We were sitting at her dining room table when she broke down and started to cry. I knew that she had lost two of her only children in the fire. She looks me straight in the eyes and said I did not kill my children. She told me that she fell asleep on the couch and woke up to the smell of smoke. She tried to get upstairs to the children's bedroom, but the fire was blocking her way. She ran out of the building and saw her husband. He had jumped out of the second-floor window. At first, she was relieved, she thought that her children had gotten out of the building with her husband. But no children, she asked her husband where the children were. He said they were sleeping on the floor next to you and thought that his wife had got them out of the building; then she remembered. But it was too late to get back in to save her family. I listened to the whole story never said a word she signed the checks and said thank you for listening to me and we hugged; I never saw her again. However, I learned a lot that day about the human emotion a fire victim goes through.

Our customers would tell me all about their stories; some were heartbreaking. But I learned how to treat the victim. I did not know it then, but we were healing the loss. They would always say John was heaven sent or God sent you to me. I taught other Adjusters about how to heal their customers. Anyone can repair a home but very few know how to handle human emotions and the trauma of loss. They needed to learn how to treat the victims of the loss while repairing the building.

It took about a year of study to be a Public Adjuster (PA). By 1992 I became a PA "Public Insurance Adjuster." Then Tom made me his small partnership in a fire restoration company, back to school again. I ended up taking 23 to 30 hours every 2 years, every 3 years an ethics class, and every 5 years an FBI background check in order to keep the license. To think I told my dad I will never go back to school. Those words, never ask what you wish for, it was all "worth It."

I had some good partners and some not-so-good partners over 35 years. I had about the fifth-largest fire restoration company in Chicago. I had partnered with a board-up company and a glass company in Franklin Park. I paid my employees very well in order to keep my competitors from stealing them from me. I trained and paid them more money than my competitors. I would take a lot of time off to enjoy the fruits of my labor. However, you must have very loyal employees to do that, you must pay them well. I did not really care so much about the money for myself. I just needed enough to live well and to get my children through college. I made sure to invest in property rentals and mutual funds for my future retirement. To think, in 1987 I read one of Trump's books and it helped me in my business. In the book, he wrote you must know what you are good at, so you must hire workers that are smarter than you in your weak areas and pay them well.

PA, Fire repair; like new again.

Now 40 Years old "What" Cancer.

It was time for my doctor's checkup appointment. I started out with Doctor D. when our children were infants. We would always talk about our children's lives and how and what they did as they were growing up. To me, he was a great and smart country type of doctor. He strongly said to me at 40 years old you would have to have a colonoscopy. I said what is that! He informed me that a camera will be inserted and go through your colon, the results should be back in about a week.

After I had seen the doctor; a week later I got the medical report. I had five cancer cells, stage 1 cancer, I was so relieved they had removed them and when they went back in, the cells were gone. I never thought cancer would come back, however, four more times in other locations over the next 30 years. We moved from Melrose Park to Addison Trail; Addison Trail High School was much better for Melissa.

These are the rocks that saved me, Melissa my second daughter was born December 23, 1985, and our first-Born Christie was born May 6, 1975. Mary and I had bought a home in Melrose Park Illinois, it was a Cape two-story, four-bedroom home on one acre. It was one of those exterior government build homes. The exterior structures were built for our WW2 Veterans; see The Post War United States, 1945-1968' The veterans paid around $4,000 for the outside completed and then had to complete the interior of the home. It was to help Veterans due to the 1929 to 1939 Great Depression, and 1945 inflation. Hundreds of thousands were built across America, and they were available for our great service men and women, GI Bill of Rights passed in 1944, about 1250 square foot homes.

About a block down Scott St "Scott St, and Fullerton Ave" there was a children's park. Mary and I would take the girls there. On the corner, there is a church FIRST BAPTIST CHURCH, of Franklin Park. This was around 1993, Melissa was around seven or so. We passed by the church going to the park. The entrance to the church had a glass front door. Melissa would stop and stare into the glass door. One morning she asked who the man in the picture was, he has long hair. I told her it was God's Son. Melissa asked, "Dad can we go in there and see him," I said not today they are closed, how about Sunday, OK.

Sunday, we got all dressed up and went. The first is a greet and meet at the church, which would be Pastor Thacker. Solid handshake, a kind peaceful, caring man; my first impression. We found a place to sit; always in the back at first. The Pastor introduces everyone and then asked newcomers for their names, where do they live, and if they would say something about themselves and their family. Time to preach all children must go to Sunday class, I sent Melissa to class. Christie was older and she stayed for the sermon. After class Melissa smiled ear to ear and was laughing, her first words were "Can we come back, Dad?"

Pastor Thacker is on the left.

Months had gone by; we had become lifetime friends. I owned a construction company. Pastor Thacker asked if I would be their custodian, I said would be honored. I already had read the bible front-to-back and thought I had an understanding and was trusted. On some Wednesday nights, Pastor Thacker would attend other churches to preach. He asked me if I would help at the bull pit and tell a story, a bible related story. I loved to go to the Upper Peninsula of Michigan, the Cisco Chain of Lakes as often as possible. Around 2 weeks before Pastor Thacker asked me to be at the pulpit, I had read a story in the Eagle River newspaper about a deadly crash. An eighteen-passenger plane had crashed, there were no passengers, just the pilot and copilot "Father and son." The plane flew from Eagle River Wisconsin to Schaumberg Regional Airport to Minocqua Wisconsin airport and then back to Eagle River, round trip charters.

At the pulpit, I started asking one of the church elders to start with prayer and their word of faith. I read at first from the bible in Mathew twenty-eight, nine through twenty. After that, I told the story I had read last week about that plane crash in Eagle River Wisconsin. The message was "Dose love last forever?" These are the words from the Father and Son from the black box of the plane that crashed. The copilot said, "Dad right engine has just cut out and stopped running" Father said "Make adjustment son" Son says "Left Engine out" Father said, "We're going down mayday-mayday." He gave out their location. I can only assume at that time he was holding his son's hand because he said I Love you son I will see you soon. His son then replied I Love you. They died in the crash; God gave them the time to say I Love you and I know they are both walking with each other besides our Heavenly Father. And that is God's grace and mercy. I then read John five, verses three through eight. Everyone there was tearing up coming up to the bull pit asking God for forgiveness, salvation, and everlasting Love. That is when I had the first opportunity to bring one of my nieces, my brother's daughter to God and his wife, and four girls were there at the church that night. Today his whole family has become powerful Christian warriors for God.

I was blessed to have worked there for around fifteen years. I had the opportunity in the summer to work with a few teens. There was this young boy of about twelve or thirteen that lived down the block from me. He would attend church with his mother on Sundays. I was a Biker and loved working on motorcycles. He would come over to my garage with his Minibike and we would work on it. His Father left his mother with no support; it was tough for them. I would tell him positive stories. I told him I had a fire restoration company and enjoyed helping others. Personally, I had witnessed a firefighter save a child from a burning building. About 2 years later the boy and his mother moved away. I always thought about him. Several years later he moved next door to one of my employees, Bob. As they were talking, he asked Bob what he did for a living. Bob said I am a salesman for a fire restoration company. He said I use to know a man that owned a fire restoration company named Marvin. Bob said I work for Marvin. Bob grew up around Western and Division St. in Chicago Il, their club was the "PVP's," Playboys, the Ventures, Pulaski Park, and gangsters. He was one of those Bad Boys. Bob got married had two boys and changed his life around to be a good man. The young man told Bob because of the friendship he had with Marvin, he had gotten married, had a child, and became a firefighter.

He worked in Stone Park. That is the next suburb over from me. I went to see him; wow GOD IS GOOD. We talked and he told me how well he was doing. **There is no such thing as a Bad Boy, we do not start out that way**.

Today, Boys Town the organization is one hundred years strong. Boys Town still follows many of the same principles and practices that originated with Father Flanagan's vision. To honor their founder, the Father Flanagan Award for Service to Youth is given to individuals who have dedicated themselves to improving the lives of children.

Let me tell you about the greatest dog in the world. Angel was born on the bad streets of Chicago about 20 years ago. She was born to spar with Pit-bulls to death. Angel was Half Pit and Half Shar-Pei recovered by the Chicago Police Department on a raid.

One morning Melissa came to me and said she found a dog that she wanted. She said, "Dad, I found this dog named Angel at a pet recovery center. I know you will not let me have her" I said, "why not." Melissa said, "You promise to keep an open mind and see her before you say no?" I said, "Yes, and why will I not let you keep her?" she said; Because Angel is half Shar-Pei and half pit bull." "Oh no, you can't have a Pit-bull" I replied. Melissa reminded me of my promise.

That Saturday Melissa was waiting for me with this big smile on her face. We jumped in the car and went off to the pet recovery center. Melissa had me wait outside while she got the dog. Angel walked next to Melissa on a leash and when they got to me, Melissa said "Sit" and Angel sat. Angel looked at me with the greatest smile I ever saw on a dog. Angel had some scars from the fighting, but I could relate to that; I also have many scars. Melissa was right, Angel was special. We adopted her and part of the deal with the recovery center was there would be 3 months of training for Melissa and Angel. Angel had to pass a test, or she would be euthanized. Every Sunday Melissa took Angel to the forest preserve with about twenty or so others for their training while I sat in the car and read a book. Angel passed the test and Melissa got to keep her.

Angel was extremely smart; one trick she did was the coolest. You point at her and say "Bang!" She would fall to the ground roll over and play dead. About every morning I would break out a treat and we would play football. I was the quarterback, and she was the receiver. She could catch that treat in midair. As far back as I can remember she would lie on the landing near the front door waiting for us to get home with unconditional love and patience.

Angel loved the Upper Peninsula of Michigan. She always knew when we were going. She would sit at the front door and wait till we packed up the car. She then ran to the car and stood at the door to get in. That was her favorite place to be. Our home was on the Cisco Chain of Lakes on the water. We had five acres for her to play and behind us was the Ottawa forest. Angel loved walking in the woods with Melissa, swimming, and riding on the boat. If you were fishing and you cast your bobber out on the water, she would jump in the water and get it for you. I hated that but it was the coolest thing to see. I was diagnosed with cancer in 2002 and was not able to keep up the property so we sold it and bought a home on the Mississippi River.

One afternoon we packed up the car. Angel waited patiently and then ran to the car door to get in. When we arrived at the new home Angel was not so happy. The look on her face was this is not the north woods! She was sad that day. After some time, she made the place her home. The first time she jumped in the river she swam to the shoreline and got stuck in the mud. She hated that. Coney Island is a long beach that everybody goes to enjoy with their family. Coney Island is sand and no mud. Angel loved the sand on her feet. We took her there when we could.

One summer Mary and I took her to Coney. I had to pick her up and put her on the beach. You see she was 14 years old now. She was having a tough time getting around. Angel was a part of our family, and we took her everywhere. The last month she was with us we took her to Tennessee to visit relatives. We all loved her, most of all Melissa loved her and she loved Melissa. Angel had not been feeling well the last couple of days, so we took her to the hospital. We found out that her kidneys were failing, and she had full-blown cancer in her lungs. She only had a few days left to live. We took her home to say our goodbyes and try to spoil her one more time. But only eight hours later Angel died in Melissa's arms with her family by her side. We had a lot of great times with our Angel, she will be deeply missed. From rags to riches Angel, you were the best and we love you as you loved us.

Chapter 4

10 years later, cancer is back.

Our cabin on the Cisco Chain is my lifetime dream. I always had a business partner to share the risk. I made sure I was 55% owner. By being the majority owner, it keeps you in control of the business. Just smart business. In 1995, I was now looking for a retirement home in the UP of Michigan. My wife and I put a bid on five acres of property on a peninsula on Cisco Lake, off Route 2, for around $40,000 dollars. We would build a new ranch home.

About a week later, I met up with a few friends who had homes on the Cisco chain of lakes. I rented a snowmobile and remembered a cabin just down the way from the property in which I was interested. I stopped there to look through the windows and I thought I can restore this property exactly the way I want and that is what I will do. Now I had to find the owners. I found him about a month later, he was in Rockford Illinois. He had bought the property 15 years before for an investment. He was an architect in Rockford. I called and asked if you would like to sell that property. He said I just listed it with Ellison Reality Land-o-lakes Wisconsin.

I called Roy and asked him do you have this property listing on Cisco Lake. Roy informed me that it comes with two lots; one lot was seven wooded acres and the other was five acres with a cabin. What is the listing for both, he said the price is $85,00 for five acres and a cabin and the other lot is $95,000 for seven acres. I was thinking I could sell the seven-acre lot in a year or so for around $135,000 and use the extra money to pay for the restoration of the cabin located on the five acres. A problem came up; I could not afford both. So, I signed the paperwork on the cabin with the five acres; N-4032 Cisco Lake Road. I knew my wife would be so mad at me. She really deserved a brand-new home. The cabin was one bedroom with a walk-out basement to the lake; a square box type of cabin. Roy, the realtor, told me the history of this cabin. It was an old trapper cabin; the second one built on the Cisco-Chain-O-Lakes in 1906. It had a guest-type building on the property, a forty-by-forty garage with a loft, and an old Maple factory; I love that property. Now I needed to make a set of drawings of how this home would look. I would add two bedrooms and enlarge the living room and to show Mary it would be just what she wanted. I added a 12 x 10 extension to the living room, changed the shape of the cabin to an L-ranch home, added two more bedrooms, and a wrap-around deck, completely around the cabin. The property was located on Cisco Lake straight across from the Cisco Bar, perfect.

I called Mary. I told her that I have good news we can have those seven acres of land. They took our bid so we can build that house you wanted. However, I turned it down because we got a better deal. We have a cabin that was built in 1906; it is a trapper's cabin that I plan to rebuild, and closing is in 3 weeks. Holey shit: she did not speak to me till closing. I showed her what it would look like. I finely closed her on the deal; coffee is for closers Lol. Three years later, the home was restored, the garage and maple building restored, and the property was completed. I'd leave work on Monday night. I worked with Mr. Morrison and his son, then leave Thursday afternoon to work at my company from Friday to Monday. Everything was in great shape. Mary and the girls learned to love it as much as I did. Due to my cancer in 2002, Mary was not happy about retiring there.

Between 1996 to 2004 everything was going just as I planned. I made a lot of friends at Cisco Lake and Watersmeet, Michigan. There is a small casino and many nice restaurants to dine at. I met "Pate" Phillips at a golf course down the block from our home in Addison IL. Mary and I moved to Addison, Illinois in 1997. "Pate Phillips" the 80th District seat in the state House of Representatives, what a smart man. He had a home on the Cisco Chain lakes also. I would see him at Al's Cisco bar and grill playing

10 years later, cancer is back.

liars poker. No one could lie to him because he would always win. My wife and I talked with Pate and his wife for hours. I just listen to his stories and politics. We met Hollywood stars there, a lot of retired teachers, police officers, and blue-collar workers. A good friend Bob Baldassari and his family "Floors by Vincy;" his son was one of my partners, and many entrepreneurs.

Sixteen years of memories of fishing, hunting, snowmobiling, and winter sports. One morning I asked Melissa to clean the garage for me. She said I cannot Dad there is too much for me to do. I said OK; I had to think about the lesson I needed to teach her. I picked up a small ax and found a small tree to be removed. Hey Melissa, I have a small ax and we have a small tree about five inches thick that needs to be cut down; she said, "Get the chainsaw, Dad." She knew that I had cleared the property cutting down about twenty small to medium trees. I said no this is just one tree and five inches wide twenty-five-foot-high tree, and you will cut it down, it is behind the garage. I sharpened the ax and handed it to her. She said are you crazy I cannot cut that tree. I said those that cannot teach or cannot do much, take the ax, one chip at a time I showed her how to swing the ax about 2 or 3 chips out of the tree. Here you go, one chip at a time. About an hour later she came with a smile ear to ear. She said, "Dad I did it one chip at a time." I told her "That is how you will face life's challenges one chip at a time."

In 2002, I found a lump in my tonsil. I had my yearly doctor's appointment scheduled in a week for my checkup. I told Dr. Dem about the lump. He did his thing and said it is more than likely a cancer cell because of the work that you are doing. It is called firemen's cancer. My business was property fire restoration. Dr. Dem said I have a lady doctor for you to see.

I met her an hour later. She was a nice lady, but money motivated. Throughout my life, I would stay away from greedy people at all costs. She did the Biopsy and sent it to the lab. The results were available a week later. And she called me to her office saying we need to talk. I went to the appointment alone. By that time, I had done extensive research over the last several years about cancer. I had become a student of cancer; I am sharp when it comes to cancer treatments by now. She informed me that I had stage 3 cancer in my tonsil, we need to remove it asap. I asked what the survival rate is; she said about 2 years. We must operate on you within 3 days from today. I said no I am leaving I must go call my Attorney.

I called Mike D. who is a lifetime friend and my Attorney. Mike was a part of my support group also. I said Mike I have cancer with only 2 years to live. As you know I have tough business partners. I cannot let them steal from my family. We must sell all my businesses and properties asap, but we will hold onto Addison's property for now. I must make sure my family will be financially secure. The next call was to my wife, now I have tears, how I love my family so much and Mary has been my rock.

Mary asked, so what was the report? I told her it was no good. I have stage three cancer; I need surgery and they are only giving me two years to live. I heard a pause. She was at work; she was an IT specialist for Dominick Finer Foods, now Safeway Foods. OK, I will get the report from the Doctor myself she said, she is my ROCK. The next day she is on her e-mail; the crazy lady had already talked to the head pharmacist of Safeway-Foods. She sends out e-mails to fellow employees asking for their opinions or thoughts and information on doctors for neck cancer. One of the top doctors in the world just happened to be at Chicago Loyola University Hospital. Just a few miles away from my home.

I have an appointment to see Dr. P, a wonderful Italian man. He reminded me of my childhood elders, so I felt comfortable with him. He informed me the surgery must be done. However, my insurance will not cover the total cost, it would be out of pocket. Ok, I am thinking he is Italian, time to make a connection. Hey Doc, you belong to the American Italian Club. Yes, Me too. We may know the same people; I am not sure if he believed me yet. As a Public Adjuster, it was good to be a member of clubs, if possible. I was also good friends with Chicago's west side club owner of the African American club; as a member, I was able to meet a few NFL Players, the owner of Johnson & Johnson, and a member of Soul Train. I worked for Walter Payton; he was the sweetest man I ever met, and Jimmy Jones wow he had more wisdom in his little finger than most men had in their entire life.

Two Days later I was back at the university to meet with Dr P. He told me he had spoken with our friends at the American Italian club. He would

10 years later, cancer is back.

operate in two days and had an aggressive plan. Dr. P informed me the average survival is 95%!

On the day of surgery, my Wife, brother David, his wife, and my mom were at the hospital. It was an eight-hour surgery to remove the tonsil and all my left lymph nodes. Dr. Petruzelli said you will also need thirty-three radiation treatments from the nose to the top of the lungs; radiation treatment is barbaric. I had burns on my tongue, mouth, and throat. I lost my sense of taste and did not eat. Before the cancer I weighed 187 pounds and was in decent shape; after six months I was down to 132 pounds. I did not react to the radiation very well. I was in a great deal of pain. My pain medication was morphine patches. I had seven treatments left, I was so stoned I had put one too many Morphine patches on and took pain pills. I walked into the hospital so sick I thought I was going to die. My radiation Doctor was from India, he said you are going to die, you have overdosed on painkillers He rushed me in for a transfusion and liquids. I got upstairs around 2 p.m. and stayed for about 3 hours. He came to check on me and said no more radiation. I said you are wrong we will finish this, please have the machine ready tonight, he said OK.

My choice: I had to stop taking pain meds that night. The body can put off the pain by sending releases on its own. The last seven days of radiation felt like it would never end. Three days after my last radiation treatment my daughter Christie had a baby Girl. They named her after me and my wife "Samantha Ann" my middle name "Samuel" Mary's middle name "Ann." Christie's new last name was "Ramirez." Christie had married a hard-working caring wonderful man who came from Colombia at the age of sixteen with dual citizenship.

I told my wife we're going to drive this Motorcycle to the hospital, she freaked out, but always supported me. Off we went, she had to hold the bike up for me so that we would not fall over when we stopped. We made it to the hospital to see our granddaughter and back home through God's Grace. About five years later Dr. P moved to Georgia to teach and complete his career.

Call On God

My cancer recovery would take 4 years. Three days after my last radiation treatment Mary took me per my request to Cisco-Chain Cabin. Mary and I were on our way to the cabin, this was a good and happy day for me. I had bought her a convertible some years earlier. I was thin, underweight, weak, hundred-thirty-two pounds, and always cold. The drive was three hundred-ninety-six miles from home to the Cabin, about seven hours one way. About halfway there I could not take it anymore. She was driving her new convertible and was happy on that day. It was around 90 degrees; I was very cold. I asked Mary please close the top and turn on the heat, you had to see her face, priceless. We were on Route 45 just north of Eagle River Wisconsin. Eddy K. owned property and storage units; he was having a garage sale. We stopped to visit Eddy; he had a single-shot 1950 Sears twelve-gage shotgun. I paid fifty dollars for the gun and talked for a few minutes. He said I looked great. He always had nice things to say. He was a Chicago entrepreneur; and salesman, and he was able to turn shit into money.

Mary took us to the cabin. My goal was to sleep and eat so that I could recover from the radiation treatments, drugs, and weight loss. Mary stayed about a week and a half. I was not ready to go home. Terry S. owned the cabin next door. It was the first cabin built on the Cisco Chain; it was an old logger's cabin built around 1901. We were partners and had investment properties around the area together. We became great friends. He purchased the cabin in 1998. Terry's business was in downtown Chicago, "Midwest Gold Stamper" and did very well for himself. He told Mary he would take over my care for the next 2 to 3 weeks as needed. About 4 or 5 days had passed by. Terry would cook for me and help around the cabin. I was taking a nap on the couch when I heard this deep voice "GET UP YOU NEED TO GO FISHING," I knew it was God. I got up walked over to Terry's cabin and knocked on the door, Terry said "Marvin what the hell are you doing," I told him you must take me on the boat, I must go fishing right now. Without skipping a beat, Terry was all over it. We went out about five hundred yards and threw out a fishing line for about 15 minutes. I said I am done please take me back.

10 years later, cancer is back.

The next day I got up and made my own breakfast. I just started feeling much better every day, as if Jesus had been caring for me all the time. I just did not know it, "Jesus's footprint was in the sand, he was always there, Jesus has been carrying me for the last 8 months". Two weeks had gone by; I asked Terry to take me home. I read a book the first one ever that was not a motivational book or the Bible. The book "Holes". Wow, that is what I have been missing. Love that book, my daughter got it for me, then another book 'Five people you will meet when you die' is another great book.

The recovery was terribly slow because 2 years later I was about 150 pounds. I was alone in the cabin. The family had left the day before. I had a flat-bottom fishing boat that I no longer needed. I asked Al if he would like to buy it. He said to bring it to the bar. I got there around 3 pm. I used the ATV the kids were playing and driving with around the trails behind the cabin with the neighbors. I forgot to release the brakes for the kids. The bar was down the gravel road about three miles. When I got to the bar parking lot, I tried to stop, the brakes did not work. They were worn and needed to be adjusted. All I had to do is turn an adjustment screw-up before I was to leave. Eddy K. was at the bar with his family; I had a couple of beers with them and others. I wanted to do some fishing in the afternoon, it was around 5:30 pm I had to leave. I said my goodbyes. It was a strange moment for me, Eddy gave me a long Kiss on my lips and with sad eyes. He said I Love you Marv, eight months later he would die of throat cancer.

I had purchased a dozen worms; I left the bar; I did not put my helmet on. I forgot to tighten up the brakes and I put the worms between my legs instead of the glove box where they belonged. I went on my way. I was on top of a small hill-like bluff. I was on a dirt road on the left side and it was around a turn I lost control. I went down the hilly bluff, hit two trees, cracked my skull, and broke two ribs in my back. I was knocked out. I woke up before sunset, stood up, and then passed out. The second time I got on my knees and passed out again. The third time the sun was just starting to set around 8 pm. I stayed on my knees. I checked myself, there was blood all over my short pants and my hands were full of blood. It was time to pray and ask God for some help. My prayer was please God do not let the Bear or that Wolf eat my face if I die tonight. I would like my family to see my face. I knew by morning if I were alive, I would be able to climb up the hill to the street.

At Al's Bar & Grill, there was a mother-daughter team spending some time together having a few drinks. It was around 10 pm they had to make a choice of what road to take. They lived south of Thousand Island Lake, on Thousand Lake Road. The mom said we should drive around the dirt road and around the lakes to get home, her daughter said it is faster to take Route 2; faster and safer.

Her daughter said, "Let's take Route Two,", her mother said "no there is a new lady sheriff waiting on Route Two giving out DUIs. Let us just take the dirt road around the lakes in order to get home." They decided to take the backroads. As they got around the first turn her mother saw a red light in the woods and said to her daughter there is a red light and said look down there, we need to see what it is. Her daughter said no I do not think it is anything. However, they walked down the hill and they found me. They knew me and I was badly hurt. By God's Grace, he makes miracles. The mom is a nurse, and the daughter is a Watersmeet Michigan, EMT, I am saved again.

My brother David owned a bar restaurant in Watersmeet across from the Lac Vieux Desert Resort Casino and Reservation the Chippewa Indian Committee. The Lady Nurse called David and Al and said get down here now Marvin crashed into a tree with the ATV. I do not think he is going to make it; we cannot get the ambulance because the driver is drunk from Watersmeet Michigan. Finally, they got an ambulance from Conover Wisconsin about twenty miles away. They took me to the Eagle River Hospital fifty-two miles away. I received about thirty stitches to fix me up; I also had a cracked skull.

David called my wife and kids who were back home in Glendale Heights Illinois. They were about three hundred miles away. Mary walks into the hospital room looks at me, the first thing she said you are supposed to be dead, I said Not today,

Four years after the cancer, my weight was 167 pounds and that was where I would stay. I felt good at that weight. Mary my Rock said we must sell the cabin, there aren't any specialized cancer hospitals nearby. I was heartbroken, this was to be my forever retirement home. She said it is because you cannot take care of it anymore and I know I was in denial. We cannot retire here because the hospitals in the upper part of Michigan were small towns and not up to date on cancer and cancer treatments. It broke my heart, but I knew God had a plan, I was well; live with it! I also sold all our other investment properties. Terry still has his cabin and I go there often. He made a spot for my motorhome with water and electric hookups. He also has a 2-bedroom, one-bath cabin and a 2-bedroom, one bath above the garage and a pontoon boat; Life is Good.

Chapter 5

Harley Bike Trip around Lake Michigan

A Harley Davidson Bike Trip around Lake Michigan in 2014; was one of many on my bucket list. I enjoyed belonging to the Harley Wild Hogs. We had about three hundred members that were mostly veterans. For the trip around Lake Michigan, I made the routes and all the stops for this trip. Pickup locations, lunch stops, gas stops, and dinner including motels. I am the captain and safety captain, can you imagine that, Lol. It is a Friday, a three- and half-day trip. I will pick up my brother Robert and his son Paul, on North Ave and Schmale Rd. My next stop would be Indiana to pick up our rear captain Steven and a friend. We get there at 11 am just in time. We must leave by 12 O'clock so we can get to the motel before dusk to avoid bears and deer crossing the road. Yep, Steve is always late, over an hour. Robert said why are we waiting for Steve you never ever waited before, you should always make a plan and always stick to it, for safety reasons, let's go. Right then Steven shows up, but without the other rider. We did our safety checks and then we were on our way. It is about 1 o'clock now and we were running late. There is this cool Harley Restaurant on the way and we have no time to stop. It is about 6:30 pm, Steve and Paul said to me they were starving and insisted that we stop for a late dinner. I knew better than to stop, but I did it anyway. Remember those last few words I said, "Make a plan and always stick to it."

Life has its choices and there are always consequences. I had most of my crash gear on, it is now dusk. I pulled us off the road to make sure everybody had their crash gear on. I am wearing a 1930 helmet mostly made of rubber.

I looked at my real helmet sitting on the passenger seat then looked at the map, we're only thirteen miles from the motel. I decided I will not need that helmet. We are on the move after everyone had their gear on. We were about a mile down the road when Steve pulled up on my left flank. I thought there must be a problem; it is dangerous for the front captain to be to the front right side of the road; your vision is impaired. Now I am waving my left arm to Steve to move, back off. We were doing around fifty miles an hour when a deer came out of the woods; coming fast. I am on the brakes hard and just missed the deer. I slow down around thirty-five miles per hour for about fifty feet because there is always a second or possibly third deer; I think it is safe now, gas-on. Shit, I am going to be T boned by another deer. I cover my head with my hands and jumped off the bike a second before the dear T boned the bike, now I am flying. I landed on my head cracked my skull again, and broke my sternum end to end 'I am not breathing'.

Paul said, "Dad Uncle Marv is not breathing help me." Paul turns me over and knows what is happening. Paul put his foot under my back by my spine, places his hands on my shoulders, and pushed down. What he did was open my rib cage and open my sternum; I started breathing again. Steve's job was to stop traffic and Robert was to call 911. EMS was the first to show up. It just so happened to be two ladies on their Harley bikes; how cool is that? They removed my leathers very carefully, but they cut my clothes off, brand new pair of Harley jeans and my favorite white Harley shirt; at least they saved the leathers. They took me to the hospital, and I am awake. I had severe bleeding in the brain, and they cannot help me. They wanted to transfer me by helicopter to a hospital in Lower Michigan. The helicopter was canceled due to high winds and heavy fog.

It will be a three-hour ride in an ambulance for me. I hear the EMS Fire Fighter saying, "Stay with Marvin Stay with me," I looked up and then say, "Hey I'm Not Dying today, I just need some rest." "No sleeping," he tells me. He talked to me for 3 hours. I keep saying "Are we there yet," LOL he smiles.

The doctor in the small town where I was first taken told my wife not to rush to the next hospital because he is not going to make it. Mary asked if I was awake and coherent, Doctor said yes. Mary said, "he is not dying today sir." I am at the hospital now in an induced coma for three days in order to relieve the blood pooling in the brain. The doctors said I must stay in intensive care until the bleeding stops. I was in intensive care for about a week then moved over to another room for three weeks. I was out of there in about four weeks. I was transferred to Marion Joy in Illinois. What a great rehabilitation hospital. I had a ball there with lots of pranks and jokes. However, they were serious and well-educated in their craft. To make a long story short, I was told I may not be able to walk safely by myself, speak well, or even do small things like cooking, problem-solving, taking baths, and so forth. I am in the hospital for seven weeks. After seven weeks, I was at 60% of brain function. As of 2017 a few years later my brain had recovered to a full 96% of brain function.

Oh no! Cancer Again, I cannot believe it. I was given a lot of blood tests due to my PH levels being high. They started checking them weekly. The doctor informed me that my PH levels were very high and going up with each blood test. It is probably Prostate cancer.

The third cancer was found, Prostate cancer. I was at Marion Joy in rehab when they found Prostate cancer. He tells me not to worry one out of four men get it. It is time for me to do more research on cancer. The doctor, in my opinion, is another Money Greedy Guy, I caught him off guard when I said, "Look this is a hospital, it is a business, it is all about making money, just say what it is". He tells me his plan even before they do the biopsy. How dumb am I? I said we need a biopsy to confirm how many tumors, how large they are and exactly where. He orders the biopsy about a week later. I met with him a week after the tests and informed me that I have five cancer cells, one is about three centimeters in stage two, and two are about two centimeters at stage one. What are my options; he said we can remove them with surgery. Survival is 78% and your out-of-pocket cost is about $20,000 dollars. Option two is a radiation seed that we plant in your prostate. The survival rate is 72% and your out-of-pocket cost is about $12,000 dollars. He does not know that I have done the research and found specialists regarding Prostate cancer,

I asked him about proton beam therapy. He said that was too new of a procedure and he did not recommend it. I stood up and said goodbye doctor. I had already talked to a top proton beam therapist in Texas; they had a perfect 100% survival rate. Very costly and the Insurance would not pay the full amount. However, we can work it out. I made an appointment with a truthful easy speaking doctor at Northwestern Medicine in Illinois; they had a state-of-the-art proton system, Proton therapy precisely conforms to the shape of the tumor, resulting in less damage to the surrounding areas of the tumor. Their survival rate was 96%, good enough for me. What will my cost be, he said you will need thirty-three treatments at your cost of about $10,000 each, that is if the Insurance will pay. The insurance company does not like the cost, I said I am a PA, and together we can get them to pay.

Ok my first letter and only one with my doctor explaining why proton is the best option.

"Dear Sir,

In the event cancer returns doing either an operation or radiation seed, your insurance company will have paid for it twice. I am a PA, it is a fact the survival rate for the two procedures is very low, 72% survival and a high degree of a return of cancer cells. Cost versus Value, you can save money and pay more in the long run or pay for the value one time. You have a fiduciary duty by law if the cancer comes back. I will sue your company for the full cost of the treatment plus other damage, this can be in the millions. Are you willing to take that chance?"

My doctor called them and followed the plan. The insurance company conceded and agreed to pay the entire bill in full. Hard work, always do your research, it is your responsibility to take care of yourself, God gave us all this free will.

The cancer is gone, it has been over 10 years now and there have been no problems. In 2021 my son-in-law was diagnosed with prostate cancer. I gave him all the research that I knew of. I asked my daughter Christie for him and her to include his complete family. They must have a family meeting and talk about the plans that would be best for Luis. He will need all their love and support, lots of hugs and kisses, and the power of prayer, and with

Faith, there is always Hope. Luis Ramirez's family loves God and are church-going Christians, which is the key to survival. Luis's union insurance paid for the Proton therapy.

I learned back in 2002 it is important that you take responsibility for your health. I always had smarter people around me, I knew my weaknesses and strengths do all the research ask others including family friends, and those you met that may have gone through cancer don't be afraid to ask questions and seek other doctors' opinions. It is your life, and you know your body better than anyone else. It is ok to research alternative medicines, procedures, hospitals, and Doctors. You don't have to rely on one doctor's decision.

"Fourth cancer and it is pissing me off." Now there is this Covid in America. Unless you had Covid symptoms the hospitals would not see you. I am sick, there is something stopping me from swallowing at times and breathing becomes short when I am doing difficult tasks. I am very tired, sleeping most of the days. I called my new doctor, the one I had gotten when we moved to Clinton Iowa. My wife takes care of everything, including providing all my health records for doctor's appointments, medicines, and so forth. They will not see me; they are only seeing people that may have Covid symptoms. In February 2020, it started, a few months later I told my wife I need to see the Doctor. I need some help because there is something wrong with me. She called Mercy Medical Associates they said I cannot go to the Hospital, but they would take a swab test. I said for what, without looking at me or testing me, my doctor gave me an inhaler to use. Dumbass he knew I had cancer three times before, however, it seemed to help me. Every summer for the last 7 years Mary and I have traveled to Florida. We started going to Panama City for a month, by 2020 we purchased a class C motorhome, and we are staying for 1 to 2 months.

Around July, five months later, it was getting worse. Mary finely got me an appointment. First, I had to go to the Mercy one drive though for a covid test. They would not give me an appointment to see the doctor without it. I have been in lockdown for 6 months what the hell.? I am pissed off, I believe in the art of peace, and strength without violence, my wife said to me the hospital called and said you're fine, but I'm not fine. Mary called Mercy again and said I needed to see the doctor. I live right next door to Dr. Saadi, a heart surgeon on the Mississippi River. He is Iowa's top heart surgeon. We have become very good friends. Mary kept pushing me to talk to our neighbor; by now she had enough. MARY SAID GO TALK TO Dr. Saadi, I said when I see him I will. That Saturday he is working at the riverfront, of his home. I said, "Hi Doc, how are you?" Saadi said "Good Marvin, you?" I replied, "Doc do you have a moment to talk?" Doc always has time for you. I informed him that I have a problem with my doctor at Mercy One. I told him what had been happening for the last 8 months. I told him my symptoms. He said you have cancer again. He said on Monday at 8 am go to Mercy they will be expecting you; we will have you ready to go to Davenport Hospital for a CT scan.

Mary and I went to Davenport for the doctor's appointment. He used a camera scope first in my throat. He saw a 2 cm spot on my left vocal cord. He informs me that a biopsy is needed. During the biopsy, he nicks a blood vein. I started bleeding not too badly; he got the sample and sent it off. Over the weekend, we met up with Melissa, Luke, and his sister's family at a place called Tunnel Trail Campground in Wisconsin; 3 days of biking. On Saturday while having lunch I got something stuck on the blood vessel, I started bleeding and was not able to stop. I said to Luke, my son-in-law, take me to the hospital, I cannot stop the bleeding. I had just filled a 5 oz cup with blood. We got to a small-town hospital, they were able to get the bleeding under control, I thought things would be ok.

We had an appointment At Iowa City University for a CT scan. I have done all the research needed to make good choices. Iowa City University is the third top Cancer Hospital in the United States. Dr. Laux is the top best cancer doctor in the US, a no-brainer. He was going to look at my lungs. They found two cancer cells in there; one cancer cell on my vocal cord was about 2 cm and one cell behind my thyroid was three centimeters and stage 3, plus about the size of a ping pong ball. He said we will do another biopsy on that large tumor. This time they cut a blood vessel, and there was blood everywhere, they got it under control again. He told me to eat only soft food.

That weekend Melissa and Luke were coming to stay at our home for the weekend. Saturday, we had breakfast. I made my specialty Buttermilk Waffles. After breakfast, I was taking my meds and vitamins when I started choking. I pushed the air out of my lungs so hard that I broke an artery. The first time in my life I am scared, blood all over the wall, I filled a 6 oz cup; I thought I would bleed out before I got to the hospital. Before we got to Mercy One (3 miles away), they had called EMS, they put me out for the trip to Iowa City University ASAP. Dr. Saadi called to let them know I was on my way there. He had informed the throat doctor on call of my condition and all vitals; the doctor in the emergency and her team were ready for me.

I do not remember the next 3 days as I was heavily sedated. When I came around Dr. Nitin an Otolaryngologist who was to be my new tracheotomy specialist was there to see me. I needed to find out my options. Dr. Douglas E. Laux informed me; first, you need to have a trach for breathing with a balloon to stop the blood vessels from bleeding in your throat. You will not be able to speak or swallow with the trach. Second, we need to give you a feeding tube in your stomach. The doctor informed me that these items I will need for the rest of my life." I was not prepared for this, I conceded to both. That afternoon they put the trach in that has a balloon to add support for the breathing tube. They also inserted the feeding tube that is attached to my stomach. There were wires and tubes, and machines running; I looked like a living zombie.

Where do I go from here; today I feel great. However, sadness and depression. At the University, the words they would say a lot were "Quality of life at the end." Wow, on the first day that is what Otolaryngologist told me. There were heart monitors, blood monitors, needles in both arms, and a tube down to my lungs. Machines attached to me. I will spend the next 3 weeks in intensive care. My nurse was to teach me to take care of and use these new tools properly. There was a program on the wall of things they expect me to do every day, or they would take me by the hand to help me. My nurses would say things to keep me positive, Great job, you can do this, so on and so forth. On the Board on the wall, it was written I had to walk, two times a day for 15 minutes, read 12 hours a day, and shower, it was a

Call On God

list of about seven things that had to be done; but they gave you Faith and hope. I love them all.

Chapter 6

The Eighth-day, Trouble in river city

At about ten am an intern came in with students, this was common. She was the resident intern herself and said today we will be replacing the trach; it was only in about eight or so days. I could not talk, I had to write everything. I used hand gestures and wrote, "You can't do that I was told it is to be done by Dr. Nitin the Otolaryngologist only." She said no-no I will be doing it today. I don't write anything more, but I was very concerned. However, I was told the trach had a balloon that secured my blood vessel to heal so I would not bleed out; I may bleed to death. She proceeded to remove it; it was stuck. She pulled it out, hell no, shit the blood vessel had broken again. A mouth full of blood blew all over her face, the walls, and the door that was four feet away. She had a panic attack and ran asking and looking for that type of tracheotomy; she did not look at my files. The head nurse on the floor called in an emergency for the blood loss team; alarms are going off, and in seconds EMS put me out I am under. The nurses woke me the next morning and all was well. The resident intern had pushed the damaged old trach back into the spot before the EMS team got there. However, the trach gave me an infection somehow; not one but two types.

We did not know if trouble would be on its way for me, it would kill me. I got an infection on the twelfth day right under the trach. It was a little red, doctors thought it may have been from the radiation. I got home after being in the hospital for thirteen days. Two days at home my left arm and shoulder were becoming painful. I had a red streak going down from the trach in my neck to my shoulder. Five days later the pain was unbearable.

On the tenth day around my neck was blood red from what we thought was from the radiation. I told my wife I had some type of infection; the bone next to the trach looked bad. That weekend Christie came to help Mary take care of me. It was another Saturday just laying around; I am now a five feet nine inches tall zombie. Mary told Christie that she had sent some pictures of your dad's neck and chest to Iowa City Hospital through the patient's portal. The doctor on call in the cancer center said it looks like an infection. Mary makes the calls; she explains what has happened in the last 8 days. He said to bring him in as soon as possible to the emergency room. I will inform them what is happening with Marvin. We arrived at the emergency room around five pm. I laid across the chairs till around eleven pm due to two motor vehicle accidents: one involving five cars. People were brought in by helicopters and ambulances one right after another. When they finally took me into the room, the doctor said, "OK let's take a look at the problem with your leg." Mary informed them it was not my leg and showed them my neck and chest. Suddenly it went from one doctor in the room to a room full. Apparently, the receptionist at the emergency room was not paying attention to what Christie told her at check-in. She wrote down the wrong information in my chart.

They took blood, a lot of blood, and sent it to the lab for analysis. It turns out I had two extremely dangerous infections, one being a bone infection and the other a blood infection. The infections worked together and mutated. There were no drugs to clean this mess up. Dr. Laux had gotten the infectious disease team involved. They in turn called biotech chemists in Texas. A blood sample was sent to him. After receiving the sample and examining it he got on a plane that evening. Texas takes the top honors on the prestigious US News Best Hospital Rankings. All around number one hospital in the nation "GOD BLESS Texas". He had his samples of the blood tested with him. For the next three days twice a day, he took five vials of blood from me. He was making a killer drug and on the fourth day, he said we got it. They installed a pick tube from my arm to my heart; this would stay in for 5 months. Every day a Killer drug infusion; go fight do your best. I was in the contagious disease ward with all those tubes and lines again. Same routine as before; I was released 14 days later. Every morning I had to go to Mercy One in Clinton for the infusion drug and blood was sent to Texas. I love these nurses. We had fun every day for another 2 months. God is Good.

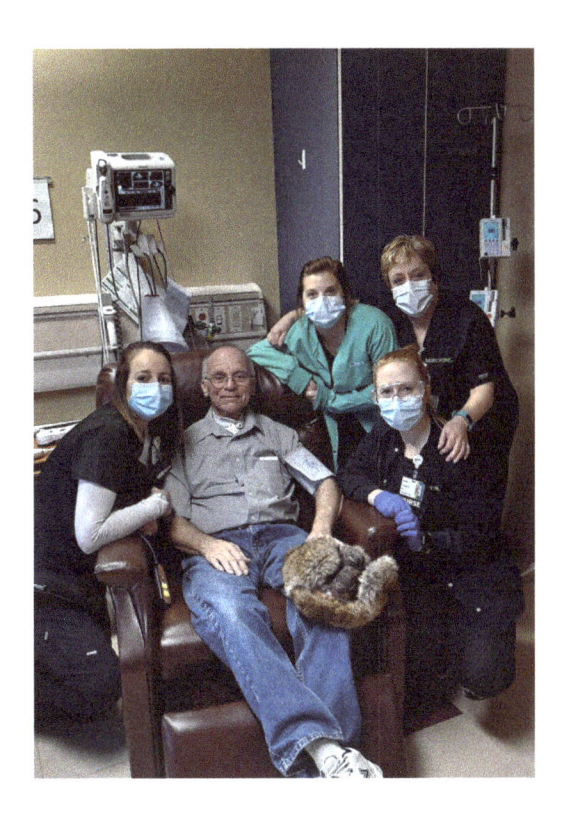

My Nurses at Mercy One Clinton Iowa.

I was not going to let all that define me. We have been going to Florida every winter for the last 7 years. We prepared the motorhome for our winter trip to Florida. I was still sick and was in the recovery stage. We stayed about two months, In February I needed to go home to rest, and I was on an exercise routine.

On the way home I started thinking about when I was in sixth grade. Like all young boys, I was in that stage between being a bad boy or a good boy. One morning I had a fight at school. We fought every day, and I got my ass beat every day. One day we got this younger substitute teacher. He had seen me through the school window. I also had anger issues. He said hey Marvin how would you like to shoot a bow and arrow; I am all over that. He said, "Do you know where the Boys club is?" It was located on Walcott Street by Walcott School. I was there that Wednesday night. When I arrived, he was there to meet me. He was one of those big brothers for boys, hell I did not care. Bow and arrow were the only things on my mind. He showed me around the place. It had everything pool tables, a pool, all kinds of games to play, and boxing. Everything you can imagine for a young boy. He taught me how to use a bow and arrow for the next hour. This was the start of a new look at what things can be for my life. After he told me some things about himself, and how he overcame his problems in his childhood growing up he told me to be back on Friday.

We started at the library, "hell no not for me." I am sick of school. He said we are going to teach you something new tonight, it was a Friday. I have something I would like to show you, sure ok. I saw a game called chess. I did not even know what checkers was, I live in poverty. I said no, and he told me to leave. I was stunned. I said, "What, never mind I will learn Chess." Another great night. Big brother said to come back next Wednesday. I got there early I was so excited. We went down to the basement; it was boxing today. We are going to teach you to fight properly, then Karate. For the next seven years, I had six golden glove bouts with two wins. I studied Karate from twelve till around sixteen years old. It was the stretching exercise routine that I liked the most, which I really did all the time. I still do that routine for about a half hour to an hour every other day it gives me peace, and solitude and fills my soul with faith that I can overcome Life's hard knocks.

I met my wife Mary Ann right on Lee ST., between Hoyne Ave. and Damen Ave. I was sixteen and a half years old, and it was a nice summer day. On the steps of a three-flat building sat Mary Ann. She was visiting her sister who had moved there a few weeks prior. In the picture below my dad is sitting on those steps. My Dad would walk my mom's dog there. How ironic that I would fall in love, at first sight, where my Dad had someone take pictures of him. She was sitting on the top step, the steps my dad was leaning on. Do you believe God always has a plan; just go with it.

Mary and I dated for two and a half years. She lived on the corner of Augusta Ave. and Western Ave. Her family lived on the second-floor three-bedroom apartment with two brothers. On the first floor was a store that sold poultry and live chickens. Mary had her very own live rooster on their back porch, crazy.

I would walk her home. When we had a few pennies, I would buy an order of French fries; they were five cents. She still loves fries today; it was simpler times. Sometimes we would stop at the Chicago Pizza place and get gravy bread for ten cents for two pieces. We ate a lot of beans and cornbread those days. My Mom would make a gallon of beans and a pound of cornbread. Our breakfast was buttermilk and cornbread in a glass. Our steak dinner was white bread with her homemade chicken gravy over the top and beans. I still have all my teeth thanks to that. That was the same for Mary's family.

Mary wanted to be a cosmetologist. She went to a top Chicago School and got a job at Saks Fifth Avenue Luxury Fashion & Designer Clothing store. Her clients were newscasters, some tv stars, and high-profile Chicago women; she hated it. Back to a small college, then she found her lifetime job. Mary went to work at Dominick's Finer Foods, a family-owned business at the time. She met Mr. D "Dominick's Finer Foods," Mr. D was a very down-to-earth type of person. You could often see him sitting with his employees outside on break or in the cafeteria. He knew most of his employees by name. While working at Dominick's she had become friends with Mr. Mariano. At the beginning he was in the office Deli department and at the end was the CEO of Dominick's. Mr. Mariano became the CEO of Mariano's Grocery Market after leaving Dominick's. We are on a mission to help create communities free of hunger and waste.

Christie had a tough time learning in school. It took some time for us to get her a tutor, which helped a lot, she and I are a lot alike. We would bring every book home, spend hours working on homework, and still just get a passing grade. It was frustrating for her, and I understood the pain. It was the same for me. She was a great athlete. Mary started Christie swimming at around six years old. In backstroke, she won state, and her goal was to go to the Olympics someday. When she graduated high school, she went on to attend Stevens Point University in Wisconsin. She started out to be a forest ranger. She had all her classes ready for the first day; the talk about policing part, she said Hell no not for me. She called crying and wanted to come home now. She said she had made a mistake. I told her you can, you will, you must succeed, and talk to your counselors. She started over; she loved the new studies, five years, and about $65,000 in loans. I only helped a little, you must put skin in the game or there is no value, no incentives to be the best of what you can be. Life was not meant to be easy.

As for Melissa, we learned from our mistake with Christie. We hired a Catholic school teacher to tutor Melissa. The best thing we ever did. All children are smart, they just need a little help. She attended Addison Trail High School. Just like her sister, she also was a fast swimmer. However, she did not care about winning. I took her to golf lessons she loves it. One afternoon we were golfing in Addison, Illinois. Melissa's high school coach Mr. Yacino (bowling) saw her on the golf course with me. Melissa's bowling average is 185. Mr. Yacino, the boy's golf coach was practicing with his team. We were at the second hole a par three, Melissa nails it. Next a par four, Melissa nails it. He pulls up next to us on a golf cart. The coach said, "Hey Melissa would you like to be on the girl's golf team?" He had already contacted the girl's coach about Melissa.

Mr. Yacino went to Western Illinois University and Melissa wanted to go there also. She got some grants, worked a school job, and ended up with about $60,000 in loans. The summers she worked with me learning to be a PA. She learned to do property damage estimates and personal property inventory. She started her own IRA at the age of 17 years old. She was already a good investor; she was a great student. She had more credits which helped her get her master's in one and a half years. Now working for ABC, she is a manager in accounting; permits, and taxes.

Chapter 7

5th time for cancer, Brain cancer

I was on my way back to Iowa City University for a routine CT scan. It was my fifth time being diagnosed with cancer. It would be Brain cancer about three-quarters of an inch in size or two centimeters on my left temporal lobe. The CT scan also revealed I had one in the upper part of my lung also about two centimeters with both being stage two. I am sixty-seven years old now. I thought I was home-free after the fourth cancer diagnosis. My Prayer was this:

"Dear Heavenly Father, please do not let me die of Cancer and die in pain. It is too great, just let me have a natural death. I see the process in other cancer patients; it is demeaning and painful. Please let me fall asleep, put on my carpenter pouch, and build homes for Your children in Heaven; not so much to ask; Amen."

Dr. Laux has the best cancer team in the US. It was November 12, 2021 and time for my checkup with my head doctor to include a CT scan. About an hour later I got the report, another tumor. Within an hour he had scheduled an MRI for accuracy. I have a tumor on the front part of the brain next to the skull above the left eye and one in the upper lung more likely it is cancer. A couple of days later we went back to the hospital in Iowa City. The brain and lung cells were around two centimeters. I would have to meet with the doctors to plan. Mary and I met with Dr. Greenlee concerning the brain tumor, he had a couple of options. For this type of brain tumor, there were two ways to deal with it. First was radiation, with a low survival rate. However, you would be able to have radiation whenever it was needed; it was targeted therapy. Dr. Greenlee believed that the tumor had not gotten into the brain. It was located on the outside next to my skull. It would be an easy surgery and more than likely, he would remove the entire tumor. With surgery, I would only need one radiation treatment, for a survival rate of ninety-six percent. The radiation was in order to make sure there were no live cells. However, as for the tumor in the lung, we needed to know what type of cancer it was. Once the brain surgery was done, they would test the tumor mass; to make the next plan. They believed I would need to go back on Keytruda; that would be our next plan. However, you would be on it for the next two years. If Keytruda did not work, then they would do chemotherapy.

OK, I had a week to research, so I could make the best choice for me. Mary and I were back on our knees in prayer asking for wisdom and understanding in this new battle; God's plan was surgery. With no other option for me, we called Dr. Laux; he put together his team of warriors to work on the plan and schedule. I had a reconstructive surgeon, who would oversee the surgery; an anesthesiologist who would oversee perioperative care; another who would oversee the radiation, and one that did the micrographic part of the surgery, with a team of nurses.

Friday, November 21, 2021, is the big day. I am now strong and in good shape, I've got this. They said after surgery I will be in the hospital for a day for recovery. I said I will be out the next day. The doctor just smiled and said, "With you anything has been possible." The surgery started at Ten am sharp and was over five hours later. It was just what they said easy peasy. Once out of recovery and on the floor, I was so hungry my nurses only had one patient that was me, I called for food; wow anything I wanted. Ms. Amy said the restaurant closes at six pm. They have a great cook also in the University, I did not know that. At ten pm Amy said I am going down to get something to eat do you need anything. I gave her a list. She said to me are you planning to eat all night, I said yep glad to be alive.

The next morning at six am I ordered a large breakfast. I was feeling great as if I were 40 years old again. My nurse came in to check on me, I asked her if after I clean up if I could walk around, and she said we will see. In the next bed over, there was this young man that had an auto accident. He was thrown out the front windshield of his automobile. He had to have major brain surgery; cut, removal, and replacement of his skull on the right side from the front around and down to the lower part of his ear, about sixty stitches, and five staples. He almost did not make it at all. He was in a great deal of pain all night; I felt so bad for him. I prayed for him all night long, I ask God to make me his tool to console this young man. The young man was mad, scared, and worrying about things that will never come about. He called his mother and father asking and begging for their help, at some point yelling why aren't you here helping me? I was sure they were in shock also. I assured him his mom and dad were doing their best, and so was he. I believed his mom and Dad were doing their best and what they were able to do.

The nurse came into the room and, she asks me how I was doing, I said all is good no worries. I got out of bed; she did not know I had been already walking around. She unhooked me from the electronics, and we took a long walk. We got back to my room, and I asked, now can I go home, she said I must call the rehab therapist first. The therapist will come and test you to make the determination. The patient in the room with me his name was Kyle. He was calling all over the town including tow companies, anybody but the right guy, trying to find his belongings. He was looking for his computer, and clothes and was saying I have to work. I prayed; God just open the door of opportunity for me to help him.

I asked Kyle what it was he did for a living and where he lived. Kyle lived in Arizona; we made small talk. He told me he had been racing. I told him at one time I had family in Mesa Arizona, in my twenties. I had run out of work and had to go to Mesa to install drywall. I sent the money back home for my wife to pay the bills and put food on the table. Kyle, you're calling people that cannot help you. I told him what I did for the last 40 years; I was a PA "Insurance Public adjuster". You need to call the county Chief the one doing the investigation where the incident happened. He will have your things. I told him before you call, I needed to enlighten you on what he will be asking you on the phone. He is going to come here to question you. Kyle asked if he should be worried and I said no.

Call On God

I said do not give the investigator too much info on the phone till you see him. I am sure he will be here on Monday, call him in about thirty minutes. Kyle do not say I am worried or scared anymore it makes you seem irresponsible. They are negative responses of guilt and not being responsible. Do not blame others for your choices, all that matters in Life is your words. I am concerned about this or that. It is a positive response; says I am responsible for everything I have done; it is believable because it happened. You are never scared, you are concerned; it is above weakness, it makes you stronger in the fight. Worried about what; when you are worried you have no Faith and with no Faith there is no HOPE.

Tell me what happened in detail, you will be under investigation by a Sheriff. You should never lie, cheat, or steal; the return will be too great for you. He told me that he stopped on Thursday at the sports bar to watch a football game. I asked if he was drinking, he said yes. Ok, he had his first drink with food, then a second one and then one more for sure. I told him to call the nurse, she can and will get you your alcohol level for when they admitted you. She can find out what it was, or alcohol limit was. So, you had four beers, maybe five in four hours. He believed I was correct. He asked me if I thought he needed an Attorney; in my opinion, I said not yet. I asked Kyle if anyone besides you got hurt/injured in the crash. You must tell the truth; the Sheriff will know the truth before he asks you the question. They will have respect for you because you give the officer respect. Be kind and caring, he may not give you a DUI in the report. He just might forget the alcohol; it does happen; It would be a believable event. The worst thing is a DUI with $1,500 dollar fine, a 1-year special Insurance cost and probation. A lawyer will cost around or about $5,000 dollars or so, remember no worries; just concerned "take responsibility for your choices" Kyle do not say words that can control you, do not let fear hurt you.

Make the call, everything will work. God has given everyone three Angels; one to guide you, one to watch over you and one to lead you. Let them do the work for you, your tonight's prayer should be three little Angels at my head, one to watch, one to pray, if I should die before I wake, one to carry my little soul away.

It will give you comfort, and you will always have your Angels in your corner. Amen

I WILL NEVER KNOW THE OUTCOME FOR KYLE BUT I DO KNOW HE WILL BE A GOOD AND BETTER MAN BECAUSE OF IT.

At about eleven thirty my lunch was delivered; lots of food on the plate and I am starving. Mary just walks in, my rock how I Love my wife; next my rehab therapist walks in asking all the questions. She says let's take a walk. She tells me I am doing great walking down the hall. Then she tells me I must walk up some stairs. We go to the entry stairway I run up two flights and down, ok I am leaving now. She is laughing aloud. She tells me "You are unbelievable it should be a three-day recovery," I say everything is believable with Faith. I eat, clean up and change my clothes; I was glad to get to go home problem free.

I am going to Florida, and I will not let cancer define me. Mary and I had to get Dr. Laux to expedite his plans. He knew that Florida was very important to us, he remembered it from the prior year. It takes almost a year to get a spot at an RV resort next to the Gulf. We needed to complete everything in 3 weeks or stand to lose some money we paid for the resort reservations. We had five reservations with our down payments made. It is very hard to get reservations; there are little or no cancelation without it costing you some or all your down payments. It stops people from overbooking at all the good resorts, leaving it hard for others to book. Our first stop is on November 1 in New Orleans. It was three days paid in advance, no money back, to include the next two of them, we are not going to make it.

Mary and I for the last 7 years had become snowbirds. We would make plans to stay by the gulf beach area in Florida for a Month or so. For the first few years, we would rent a condominium or a kitchen in a motel. About 4 years back I had this idea about a camping resort. We could have more freedom and save a sum of money by using a fifth wheel or a motorhome. It turns out we will not be able to go to Florida till December 31, 2021. However, on November 12, 2021, I have cancer. The fight plan that was needed would not be complete till around December 28th. We are right on schedule just as Dr. Laux said. Again, the man is spot on, in forty-six days he is a miracle worker. He cares for others' well-being. He told me that the first day we met was about the quality of life.

I had to start a Keytruda treatment on December 28, 2012. KEYTRUDA is an infusion that may treat certain cancers by working with your immune system. It may be used when your cancer has not spread to nearby tissue in the bladder; but is at high risk for spreading (high-risk, non-muscle invasive bladder cancer and when your tumor is a type called "carcinoma in situ."

For the next 3 years, it will take about an hour every twenty-one days to include a blood test, CT scan every 3 months. Mary and I are on a new "JOURNEY" "The End-of-Life Tour," Mary and are packing the motorhome that we upgraded in August 2021. We traded in our 28 ft Class C Plus with two slides; I will miss it. It was a little small to stay in for more than a month or two. The New Motorhome is a 33-foot class A Mirada, with two large slides, super nice and roomy with about 375 square foot living space. It will take us a couple of days to have it ready. It takes a two-night stay on the way to Crystal Isles River Florida Resort. From there we will be staying at Caladesi RV Park resort in Palm Harbor Florida, we have been trying to get in there for two and a half years, hoping to return as a Snowbird.

Chapter 8
Cancer returns 1 cell in the Brain

In June 2022, six months after the last brain cancer surgery an MRI revealed a new cancer cell. I thought I was finally cancer free, however, the cancer returned with a vengeance; the cell was about three centimeters and looked like stage three.

Again, I called on my prayer warriors, I will have brain surgery at eleven am I will need your prayers from Colombia and across America to include Facebook friends and Family. Same procedure as the previous brain cancer; but I will have multiple smaller amounts of radiation this time; all cancer cells are gone again.

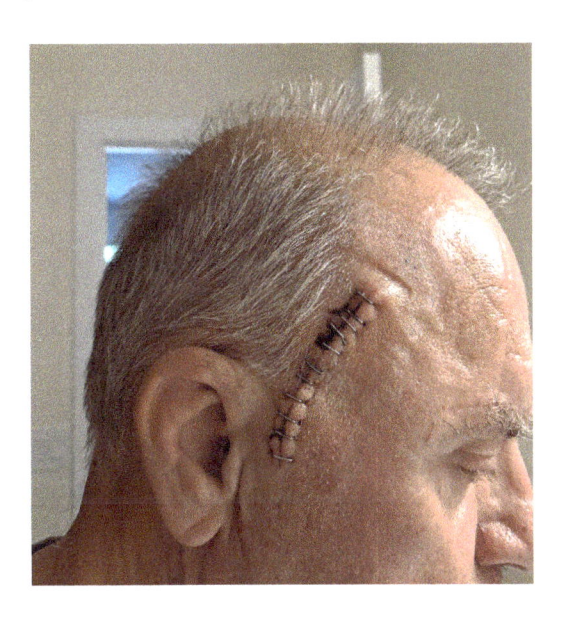

It was not so easy, I had depression; this time it was a very dark time of my life. I was depressed, mad, and frustrated that the cancer had returned. I needed help from a psychiatrist. I needed someone to talk to other than my wife.

I asked for help at the university however to no prevail. I talked to my neighbor; we had become good friends the day we moved to the new home. He told me he was seeing an older lady that treats PTSD. I met with a psychiatrist at the University of Iowa Hospital and then I talked to my neighbor's psychiatrist on the phone. I had thought to use the University's psychiatrist for one session, I thought it went well. The psychiatrist never followed though, I got more depressed. I even got to the point where I felt like I just can't seem to do the right thing, depression is real. I treated everyone that I loved as if it was their fault. I had an appointment with Dr. G the Brain surgeon. I told him what was going on. He said that the part of the brain where I had surgery and radiation (left side) Frontal Lobe, affects your short-term memory and the difference between right from wrong; that made sense to me. He said in time the brain will heal. Now I know how to move forward. I must do what I did for the brain injury I had with the motorcycle (Deer vs Bike) crash. Back to the diet and he gave me a drug that has no side effects.

The left side of the brain controls movement related to language, whereas the right side is responsible for nonverbal tasks. Collectively, the frontal lobes is the part of the brain that is home to our emotional regulation centers and controls our personality. The frontal lobes in general have a huge influence on many aspects of our intellect and behavior, evidenced by the diversity of symptoms that can occur when the area is damaged.

Cancer returns 1 cell in the Brain

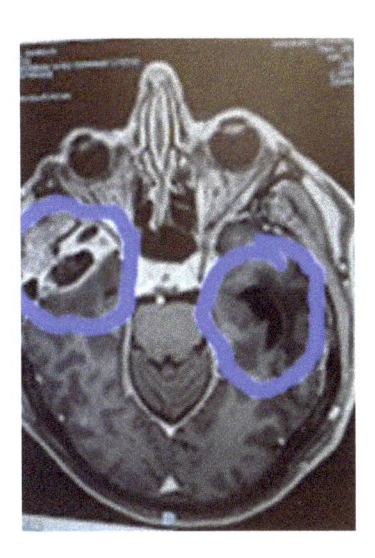

Left circle is the second brain surgery area and one on the right is the Deer VS Motorcycle accident.

My next thought was I need to talk to Pastor T. long-time Pastor and good friend. I started watching Inspire TV. A Pastor came on and was talking about his cancer struggling his fight, and how his faith and hope in Jesus's promises helped him through his anger and depression. Now he was cancer free for fifteen years and telling his story. I thought I have a story to tell and may help others. One morning on Inspire TV I listened to the Pastor, I downloaded his APP, and every morning and Night I would read the bible and study, God has a plan, I would say to my friends and family just trust God's plan; the plan is for you and others to know he is there for you.

My wife is the only one that can tell you what we went through, this is her account of the six months after the second brain surgery.

Mary Ann's words: "The first brain tumor Marvin had was scary, but I knew he would get through it. We were not expecting the second brain tumor at all. He did not show any outward signs of having one. When he had the second operation the doctor spoke with me afterward and said I would notice a few changes in him but no one else would. Well, we all noticed. Marvin became short-tempered, not understanding people's actions or what they were saying. Something innocent was said and he would take it the wrong way. I believe he thought the world was passing him by and needed to catch up with it. It was like that old saying "Damn the torpedoes, full speed ahead". It became very noticeable after he had the radiation treatments in that area."

"One minute he was happy then the next he was angry. Depression set in and he needed to get help. He was angry at the world, Marvin met with a psychiatrist at Iowa City Hospital. I did not go into the session with him, but he was extremely happy when he came out. He told me to cancel the appointment with the other psychiatrist and that he was happy with the one he had just seen. Marvin had only one appointment with the Iowa City psychiatrist which I thought was strange. I called the doctor's office and according to her notes that was all he needed. If Marvin wanted to see her again "he" should call her to make an appointment."

"Marvin's last MRI and CT scan at Moffitt Cancer Center in Florida showed no signs of cancer. I thought he would be happy, I was, but it seemed to depress him even more. According to the doctors, he is cancer free and has a body of a forty-year-old; not bad for a sixty-eight-year-old man. Life goes on and we can only take each day as it comes."

My lifetime prayer was always "Dear Heavenly Father, Please Make me a better husband, A better father, make me a better brother, make me a better friend, make me kind and caring patient, steadfast in all I do. AMEN in Jesus's name."

Live your journey, they are all divided up; learn to enjoy them, the good and the bad, love and loss, laughter and cry, good health and poor health, these are the things that well define us. It makes us the person we will become.

It is a new journey for us, it took two and a half years in the planning in the advent I would pass. My wife would have a home she would be able to take care of. We just sold our home on the Mississippi River; I have restored many homes for my wife. I always said someday you will have a brand-new custom-built home. It will be your design and your dream home.

This is the home we sold on the Mississippi River Pool 14, dam thirteen, we were 1.5-mile from Dam 13.

Cancer returns 1 cell in the Brain

We finished the new home for Mary. I am so proud of Mary. I honor her Love. She is my rock; I would not be the man I am today without her, mom, dad, aunts and uncles and so many others in my life. I Thank My Heavenly Father for the Gift of Life, the home was finished May 1, 2022.

Success is not defined by money, homes, and things. To define success, there is no real answer, just the way people think it is. To me success is to have loved someone, and to have been loved, to care for others, make others' lives better, to have a roof over my head, good children, to make their lives better than mine, and a family that loves me. To be happy for the choices we have made when life is upside down, there will be tough times and easy times, pain, and heartbreak, but there are greater times and happiness by staying in the game and knowing that I'm a good person. Work hard and play hard, that is success to me. Christie and Melissa, you are all those things and more, as I said many times you are my Hero. These things defined me and made me the person I have become. I have been so lucky and proud to have you for my daughters and friends.

I am now just over a year cancer free. I'm not in remission there are no cancer cells in my body, my doctor said one more year and your home free. God does answer your prayers. Being responsible for your health; being patient, being proactive in studying and researching new cancer treatments, controlling your diet, and exercising. The study, a prayer, and the bible; God's word will get you and your family through it.

Chapter 9

People that I admire.

To those that I love, they made a difference in my life; their wisdom was without measure and faith in God.

Mom: Words of wisdom

A.) Do Not Take anything from the Government, the payback is too great
B.) In a Thousand Years we will be all the same don't you worry about color.

Dad: with a great deal of integrity and honor

A) Never cheat, Never Lie, and Never Steal, if you cheat you Will be cheated upon.
B) Your mother is doing the best that she can.

C) We all make mistakes take responsibility for them you will learn from them.

Aunt Peggy and Aunt Esper

Those that I admired their Wisdom was without measure and faith in God:

Happy, Happy Girls, Mom's little sisters always smiling, Never said anything bad to or about anyone. Both believed in Mother Nature and the Creator.

Aunt Esper–"Marvin, don't eat that Bug."

Aunt Peggy–Taught me how to find wild food, clean fish and small game, I caught a rabbit by hand.

Aunt Peggy – "Marvin God gives us a Number and when your number is up, it's up!

"Make sure you will get into Heaven"

John A.

Chicago Police Officer lifetime friendship; saved my life 1969 I was 13 years old; he was the lead officer during the Black Panther raid with the FBI in Chicago.

He saved the life of a Chicago Mayor, He saved the life of a woman who was being raped in a Chicago alley. He saved countless lives as a Chicago Policemen, He was a friend to all.

My 6th grade teacher Mr. Thomas,

8th grade teacher Ms. Williams

Mike and Fredric Attorneys at Law

A Friendship from 1980

Marvin you are not a Lawyer or an Accountant

People that I admire.

Know what you are good at, Know your strength and most important; Your weaknesses.

Keep good people around you. Make sure their educated, attorneys, doctors, and accountants.

Frederick W.: we became friends in my twenties. I started spending time with himand a hand full of others. A social relationship we Played racket ball, I learned from each of them.

Loved learning their stories. Elderly Black men always told the best about the good and the Bad, I Learned the most about Real Black History though them.

2nd and 3rd generation Spaniards; that generation they talked about their fathers and mother how they were trying to find their place in America

I did not look at whites as white but saw them as Italians, Irish, Germans, Polish, Swedes, all have their different challenges and stories to tell just trying to fit in America.

One of the most important lessons in my life

This Black man was walking toward me. He was mad about something. He pulled out a pistil, he said I should shoot you; I did what he said. I was only about 14 years old I Don't remember a lot; he said sit down Kid on this porch, I did as he started to cry. He was talking about his life. I remember very little I was scared shitless he said his wife and children left him. He had lost his job, he talked for about an hour or so, I said nothing, it felt like a long time, then he just got up and said thanks, I never saw him again, that was a life lesson.

Dad was right, just shut up, you will learn a lot about people if you just listen.

Those I met that inspired me.

NFL Bears, Walter Payton, the sweetest, kindest, caring man, I ever met. He had a Limo pick up two of my employees; their husbands and wives, my wife and I. We were all treated to a night at his Night Club; All expenses paid. We sat at his table. We were escorted in by the Security Guards; treated Like Kings and Queens.

Jimmy Jones NFL Defensive and his wife Willa May had a fire in their nightclub. It took 3 days and thirty-two men for Cleanup.

Jimmy Jones Full of Wisdom Had an old soul. He also

gave me great advice on integrity, morals, and ethics.

Willa May a member of the African American

Association

Mr. Lupo the apartment I grew up in was the owner, kind and caring man.

This Doctor, that I Admire, and gave me kindness

Dr. Douglas Laux

People that I admire.

Books: That Changed My Life' and were fun

1. The King James Bible. Read it every day.
2. The Seasons of Life "Jim Rohn,"
3. Thanks to John for that Book, it truly saved my life.
4. How to win friends and influence people.
5. A Purpose Driven Life.
6. Rich Dad and Poor Dad.
7. The power of Influence. Maxwell, John C.
8. There were Lots of motivational and History Books.
9. The seven people you will meet in Heaven.
10. The Bridges of Madison County.
11. The Gospel Side of ELVIS.

Movies: I love and that made me think.

1. It's a Wonderful Life (1947)
2. Miracle on 34th Street (1946)
3. A Charlie Brown Christmas (1965)
4. Happy Gilmore,
5. the love of his grandmom.

Law Abiding Citizen.

Story of Great Sorrow and Heart Brake.

6. Master and Commander,
7. all-time best, God and Country,
8. Friendship, Loyalty, Maritime war, Navy fighting strategies beauty of the Seas.

This is Not the end of my adventures.

Printed in the USA
CPSIA information can be obtained
at www.ICGtesting.com
LVHW071603160823
755281LV00019B/631